Something for The Real to Feel

Justin E. Maclin

Publishing: Maclin Motivation, LLC

Cover Photo & Design: Mary 'MARJON' Jones

Featured Poets: Justin E. Maclin, Ambria Sylvain, Sakiya Gallon

ISBN: 978-1-71660-403-4

Table of Content

Rest in Paradise

Madea

Big Mama

Uncle Kev

Granddaddy

Erin

Uncle Jerry

Big Mel

E-Way

B- Mo

Aunt Ellen

Big Dump

Kenneth Miles

Nipsey Hussle

Katie Duncan

Kobe Bryant

John Lewis

Chadewick Boseman

Song Playlist

Running Across My Mind- Jill Scott

Like A Jungle- C-Murder

The P- Larry June

Malaysia- Premo Rice

Heartbreaker- Kaash Paige

Touch Me- Victoria Monet

Butterflies- Queen Naija

I Want To Be With You- David Ruffin

You're the One- Elaine

The Bigger Picture- Lil Baby

Jaded- Kaash Paige

Still A Thang- Snoop Dogg

Imperfect Circle- Jorja Smith

Ghetto Angels- NoCap

Why'z It So Hard- Brent Faiyaz

In The Shake Joint- Premo Rice

I Ain't Living Right- Starlito

Tomorrow Ain't Promised- Mozzy

Fine By Time- NBA Youngboy

Smoke & Maintain- Curren$y

Lonely Child- NBA Youngboy

Til Next Time Love- Larry June

Something He Can Feel- Aretha Franklin

Death Is Callin- Mozzy

Another Day in SF- Larry June

Quite Storm- Smokey Robinson

Feels Good 2 Be a Hustla- Cardo

Sentimental Mood- Phyllis Hyman

A House Is Not A Home- Luther Vandross

I Am Me

I am me.

A man stuck in his ways with a youthful demeanor, full of life and passion.

Blame it on astrology.

Resourceful, stubborn, brave, with grand passion but lacking trust and having the urge to be right.

Let not my horoscope fool you.

I'm merely a man.

A black man, a God-fearing black man who for some reason feels lied to in this world.

Lied to?

Or am I just lost in the inevitable change that comes from just living?

Is the world spinning too fast for me?

2020

Constantly being shut down by what we call the authorities.

The people who feel their blood is superior.

The hate!

Sickness oozing through the pores of the millions.

Death totals continue to rise.

Many are stuck inside while money still holds its pride.

Thoughts of conspiracy.

Are you feeling me?

Am I lost or living a lie?

These talks only scratch the surface when there's been a halt to you finding your purpose.

I'm starting to see it clearly now, 20/20 vision.

I see it.

My maturity and wisdom grows in times of woes.

Aunt passed away from cancer.

What a blow.

Moving city to city to find my flow.

Working multiple jobs but not seeing any dough.

My engagement was a no go.

To cope with the dismay, me and my homies light the dro and I still have half the year to go.

I guess that goes to show the constant flow of.... Life

Still I am me.

An everchanging me.

A man on a mission just trying to be.

Trying to be understood when no one ever could.

Trying to be loved.

You'd be surprised what can happen when someone gives you their heart and a hug.

Trying to be accepted in a country that views you as an enemy, when you're the epitome of greatness.

Trying to be all that you expect me to be.

I am just trying to be me.

I am me.

Cold Hearted

You say you miss me because you didn't hear from me today.

You say you love me but mentally I'm not here today.

What is it like for someone to not have a word to say?

To ignore your pain and just throw you away?

I'm selfish and self-centered when it comes to my feelings, emotions, and areas of life you can't relate to.

At least I talk myself into thinking you can't relate.

Night after night we fight.

You fight to get closer to me, I fight to be further away from you.

She wants to know the real me and I'm speechless because I don't know myself. She wants the love that I promised would last for infinity, but that love disappeared before the promise was made.

My track record for love was always questionable and negative but she saw the good through my errors.

What she sought out to change wasn't part of the game.

It was inevitable that what we had ended in pain.

Poor girl.

Silly me.

She wanted a warm love, filled with heated passion.

She looked for it from me.

From me….the cold hearted.

Next Time Around Love

A relationship that started with the purest of friendship.

Long days that continued to get shorter the closer we had become.

Time flew by us.

I always felt I had a lot on my plate but all the pressure I tried to keep from you.

Now I sit back in regret.

Thinking, what did I do?

You gave it all to me, you made sure I was your everything.

You gave me chance after chance, when a dog like me didn't deserve a thing.

True.

I did my best to get you anything.

The finest of restaurants, purses, even the pearls and oval shaped ring I'm sure you still have.

Now I wake up everyday alone, rethinking every relationship that went wrong.

To see everyone was a lesson all along.

Now its years later and even though we don't talk the loves greater.

Opening of the random package you sent in the mail, I couldn't help but wonder if you had the same cell.

Thoughts running through my mind I figured I would never tell.

Another failed one and my hearts first reaction was to call you.

"Hey love, how you been? Where you at? I hope you had a great day but I got a lot to say."

We catch up like old times.

I can tell you're ok but still in your head wishing you were mine.

My family is cool.

My aunt just asked about you.

She must've known it was something special between us.

Conversations you have when you know the inevitable is around the corner.

When history has taken place and you start to retrace.

Your curiosity hits the surface, trying to figure out our purpose.

Tensions rose when you started throwing sarcasm and shade at my coldhearted flaws.

Mentioning parts of me you wish you never saw.

I can tell you're still unhappy and want to get something off your chest that's been pending.

Anger resurfaces but that's one thing about me.

I refuse to argue with women.

Apologies for the pain I caused you and for all the lost time.

All that happened could be a sign.

I know you might still see me as trash, but the love is still there.

Maybe we can leave it in the past.

Lets see where it can go....next time around, love.

Black Knight (Imagine Floyd)

Here today, gone tomorrow.

A mantra we hear and see often.

Something we can understand, when it's not your life taken by another man.

To put the power of his life in someone else's hands.

To put the power of my life in someone else's hands.

To put the power of our life in someone else's hands.

A power often taken advantage of by the policemen.

The men in blue, who might be white or look just like you.

Nevertheless, fuck'em, they obviously have no clue.

To once again turn on the news and hear what they could possibly do.

Pull you out of your own car with brute force.

Don't worry about your license or insurance of course because little do you know your body will soon be another lost corpse.

They yell slurs.

Throw you on the curb, kneel on your neck, while all this time you're wondering why some think kneeling and protesting is so absurd.

No, I didn't watch it for my own mental peace, and I refuse to add it to my visual catalog of black men and black women laying dead in the street by the so call, police.

They say it was a long process and he was yelling for his mama.

He was yelling for his mama.

He was yelling for his mama!

How could you?

Why would you?

Those men in blue.

Those men in blue have no clue, and claim to protect.

Protect who?

They are just another United States joke.

Again.

He called out for his mama.

You smiled.

He asked you to stop.

"I can't breathe."

Your eyes intensified with anger and pleasure.

Two words that shouldn't coincide.

Sadly, this is all so common.

At sixteen, I wondered why my mother cried.

She was thinking I could've died.

Just an unarmed kid riding to practice.

Stopped.

Told to get out the car.

Thrown against the car.

Put in hand cuffs and put in the back of the patrol car.

Blue and white lights beaming.

I was lucky I didn't end up bleeding.

It felt normal, it was normal, for us.

Immature and naive.

Now I see why she'd cry.

Why she'd scream out of fear.

Her voice said the instructions of a lifetime.

Don't you ever do that again.

Don't you ever get out the car.

Don't you ever let go of the steering wheel.

Don't do this, don't do that.

Only thing is I'm still black.

I can sit still all I want and still get killed for that.

In the last ten years we've seen that.

Fuck a pig, fuck twelve, fuck the men in blue, fuck the swat in black, fuck a blue stripe.

At this point we know our rights here.

We have no rights here.

You wonder why we retaliate.

It's out of fear, anger, and disappointment.

Mr. Lonely (Trust Issues)

The issues of mine.

The issues of trust.

Stuck in the mental of issues I create in myself.

The loneliness I build for myself because I see my own lies in you.

Who am I to trust you, when I don't trust myself?

How can I trust you, when you've lost all trust in me?

A wall of love that you walked to but it was merely a mirage.

Someone you yearned to see and get closer to, only to find out it was
nothing.

A heart so big, you see it through my chest.

It pumps deep.

But oh, how you see the deceit.

How does something so big, so grand, be so empty?

How you were used in a bipolar play.

A mental play of two lives.

A mental play of two minds.

It may seem like I'm confiding in you to only confide in myself.

My eyes on you but I'm looking in me.

My voice projects outwardly towards your face, showing your grasp of the
inevitable content that's woven together.

Only thing is, it wasn't for you.

It wasn't to you.

Words said with little intent on you clinging to them.

All for me.

It was all for me.

For me to say, for me to hear, for me to listen, for me to understand the thoughts of me.

Not knowing the building of an emotional attachment between two people was being ignited through my thoughts.

My selfish thoughts being viewed as vulnerability to your soul.

And I wonder why it all comes to a fall.

I wonder why you have trust issues at all.

When you realized the look of hope in my eyes, the words passionately laid out weren't meant for you at all.

No wonder why I've become….. Mr. Lonely

The Calling by Ambria Sylvain

The butterflies hatch from the walls of your stomach.

They celebrate.

They dance in your solar plexus.

Flutter like butter in the microwave.

Pulling on your heart strings like utters.

The butterflies rise.

Tickle your heart chakra on the way out.

They grab your throat like a laugh.

Like a cough.

They push.

You organically sing your praise.

Like the Song of Solomon.

Solemnly declaring your love to thee.

You feel free.

And I feel afraid.

The butterflies lie forever in their cocoons.

They never hatch.

There is no butter.

I don't feel flutter.

My solar plexus crumbles under the pressure.

Dry.

Decrepit.

Logically, I ponder the validity of my joy.

If it is foolish to be so open.

Should soft words be spoken.

How do you place a boundary if everything is so scary?

My manner.

My energy.

Like blockades hoping to keep you from me.

But praying that you keep trying to come to me.

I tell you "yes" and "no" all at once.

It is white and black.

One and two.

Don't, please do.

Involuntarily I play.

If I don't then you'll abuse me.

If I don't then you might use me.

If I don't you might accuse me of not loving you hard enough.

I might not be good enough.

But I might be full enough.

Right enough.

Sweet enough.

Savory and such for your ego.

You might eat me.

You might leave me.

Falling in love is crying.

Falling in love is terrifying.

Like a different kind of dying.

Falling in love is heartbreak.

Grand Marnier' & 4Play

Something about you.

On this Grand Marnier'.

You know what I'm trying to do.

From me to you.

One cup turns to two.

Each sip from you gets us deeper.

Deeper into 4Play.

What can I say?

Let's make a switch.

Your glass for my lips.

It's going to be one of those nights.

I usually don't do this but just my luck, we both went from clueless to let's do this.

No TV's.

Couple candles.

It's a mood.

We're moving in slow motion.

My hands up and down on you.

Slow rolling in the bed as your lips are all over me.

Hold up.

Hold me.

Me gripping you.

She started up top, just to go low.

Before my eyes closed as we lay, all I see is the reflection of our 4Play glaring through the empty bottle of Grand Marnier'.

The Mac

I needed time alone, so we took a step back.

I knew what it was, so why not?

You weren't going anywhere; you told me that from the start.

I prayed on your insecurities and your love in me.

Made you forget about all your beauty, even though you were too good for me.

I know you're trying to settle down but just chill.

Eventually I'll come around.

Just don't decide to leave to soon.

The calls and texts were always an instant reply.

Baby come through and let's talk for a minute.

The bond we got is limitless.

Mind altering conversation to stimulate your expectation.

What are you doing this weekend?

I'm going to be taking a trip across the boot, so it's only right that I tap in with you.

I know my time has been spent sparingly but I know you respect that I'm investing in me.

No matter if I disappear and be on some other shit, when we reconnect that flames going to appear.

No fear.

She said your communication is hazy but it's crazy how you make me.

Face to face, you're never lazy.

When we're apart I often contemplate, but when we're together, I open up, I open you up, and I see your soul.

Your amazement.

She said I can't help but feel this is heaven sent.

Vulnerable she is.

Mine she was.

Together forever we will be.

Intertwined in the web of the Mac.

<u>4476</u>

Who would've thought I could feel this way?

You laugh at the corny things I say but how can I forget the confidence in the way your hips sway.

In a time, full of world dismay, we find joy in getting to know each other each day.

From being lost in the unknown, to being lost in time.

Hours fly by.

To being lost in each other's eyes.

Surprising blushing through your brown skin, to being lost in the comfort of each other's arms.

Yearning for your sophistication.

A beautiful site when you begin to see the shrinkage of hesitation.

In the mix of I don't know you, but I know you.

I want to see you but how to I tell you?

Don't leave me because I'm not ready to know the feeling of missing…you.

You leave but ending on the note of long-lasting hugs.

Stuck in the awkwardness of could I?

Should I?

Kiss you.

What would she do if I did?

What would I do if she let me?

Questions that need answering.

The wind of emotion when you try not to fall to fast.

Afraid to run each other away but our first conversation was about taking a weekend getaway for our birthdays.

November babies.

Many differences but many similarities.

We get spiritual and realize our palms tell the same stories.

Three palm lines.

Past, present, future.

We are in sync.

I'm not pressed but girl you got me interested.

Intrigued by what I did and didn't perceive.

I first saw you in workout leggings, sculpting a figure that was already complete.

I meet you in army fatigue, the epitome of a women filled with strength.

I locked into your effort, when we met for the drinks.

You were so beautiful I couldn't think.

I realized the game changed when you threw your hair in a ponytail for volleyball.

She's ready to compete.

That's all me.

The awareness of your complexity and flexibility.

All of this and it's only been two weeks.

Heart, body, and mind filled with nervousness, anxiousness, fear, patience, excitement, passion, curiosity.

Valid descriptions of my feelings but none bigger than hope.

Hoping I'm able to take what you give.

Hoping I'm ready for the responsibility of your expectations and class.

Hoping my patience with you allow our feelings to organically grow and last.

Hoping I don't bring the trauma from past love attachments or should I say entanglement.

Because you're deserving of the great and strait-laced.

Not to be tangled in the web of the black hearted.

I put none of this on you but on me because perfection is what I see in you.

Despite what your recollection of yourself might be.

Yes, this might be a bit much for you.

Admittedly so, I think it's corny to but these are all the thoughts I'm thinking when I dial your apartment gate code.

4476.

Bossalinie

The good dying daily.

Lives getting taken.

Hoping my times not coming soon.

Consider me and all my dogs endangered because when it comes to us in this world, we consistently get thrown the middle finger.

If it's fuck me, then it's fuck you too.

When it's all said and done, the real is going to do what he has to do.

A couple homies dead.

Bank account in the red.

Mossberg Pump laying by the bed.

Thinking, reminiscing, while the weeds roaming through my head.

Anxiety heavy in me.

Weight bearing on my chest, nights with no rest.

The folks closest to me can attest.

C-Murder said life is a jungle.

True facts from the real but still I remain humble.

I take a deep inhale of the green for my boys and family I thought would always be around.

What's lost can always be found, looking for myself as I move from town to town.

Every death and lost soul mean something, so it's a daily mission to show that every step back didn't happen for nothing.

The lesson in mistakes.

Maneuvering at a fast pace, increased heart rate on this paper chase.

Money making going up, date to date.

Martin Luther King got put down in my hometown.

So, I came up being taught to liberate and never sulk in defeat.

Hard body, built tough because where I'm from we don't feel sorry for the weak.

Sometimes you might have a blunder but stay cool and maintain.

Keep your head above water and never go under.

For all my homies, hustling and feels like you aren't gaining traction, keep going.

Your time is right around the corner.
For all my ladies looking for love in all the wrong places.

Dreading having to look in the eyes of these strange faces.

Keep your heart.

Never let it close for business.

For all my folks not here with us anymore, we're going to continue to blow smoke for you.

We miss y'all, we miss y'all.

For everybody else.

Keep living.

Keep moving forward and progressing.

Thank God for your blessings.

The goal is to live a fulfilling life and feel lavish.

Remain humble and pay homage to those who paved the foundation for your creations.

Bossalinie.

She Said It…. So It Must Be True

She said it, so it must be true.

The things that we have in common are more than a few.

Our skepticism of people we're interested in.

True.

The need to dive deeper into one another.

True.

We have put-put bodies that need extra maintenance, or they become struggle-some.

True.

Our interest in travel and not living in our home states.

True.

Our need to not have connectionless rough sex.

True.

Adoption views and the need to give back.

True.

Panic and anxiety attacks.

True.

Being lovers.

True.

Views on sexual freedom and the empowerment of women.

True.

Life pushed us to therapy.

True.

We search for deep connection, but those connections scare us.

True.

Understanding the importance of emotional and mental health.

True.

Writing and maybe singing.

(She thinks I have a captivating voice.)

True.

The importance of spiritual practice is there.

True.

Being cultured and the relevance of it.

True.

We both come from split families with parents who remarried.

True.

The single mother experience is greatly appreciated.

True.

Seekers.

The pursuit of deeper thought.

True.

Food.

Let's go eat!

True.

But the question remains, am I meant for you?

Can we take us two and become one combined body with the same hue?

Stuck together like old elementary school glue.

So sick in love, like we caught a new strand of the flu.

Endless opportunities in these similarities because I know you feel the same way.

The Dumpster -Sakiya Gallon

Aunt what's that?

"That's the dumpster" she said

The dumpster bangs at night

By morning someone's dead

In 5th grade my uncle got shot in the leg

But a girl in my class said her uncle got shot dead

I heard banging last night and wondered what it was

But my aunt said it's the dumpster so in her I trust

In 6th grade some kids around my way got ambushed and shot and their
house

After that I had to go to school and come home; I wasn't allowed to go out

A bullet went through the window of a house and killed a girl on her couch

Crabs in the barrel trynna climb their way out

They found my cousin's best friend with a bullet in his head

The corner near my school was running with red

Chiraq, New Warleans, Killadelphia its all the same

Hollow shells with deep pain float through the air without a name

Before I Walk Out of Your Life

Here we go again.

The phone rings over and over.

Memories going through my mind.

A big unrest.

A broken heart.

An innocent soul torn apart.

At first, I wanted to make things right.

Thinking of your smile.

Unlimited good times.

Best friends.

Lovers.

We started rocky.

Friends switching to lovers.

I felt like I never completely had your heart from the start.

How do you blend this?

We did.

I promised to never cause you any pain.

A failed promise.

I betrayed you.

You never expected it.

Of course, I want to go back to being the same.

As you now know…. I cheated.

Unfaithful.

Real nigga.

So, I charged it to the game.

The look in your face was a sight I'll never forget.

Imprinted in my brain for a lifetime.

You were defeated.

Mislead.

You saw the ugly in me.

Word for word, from the opposing side.

Somehow you still tried to fight and maintain me being yours and you being mine.

Hurting you, hurt me more than it seemed to hurt you.

I couldn't stand to do this again.

I know where you stand.

I know the love you have for me.

But I don't trust myself.

I don't see how you can still want me.

You were everything to me.

Yet, I still lie.

I still cheat.

I tend to be there but not emotionally around.

You proved to be down.

Even when I chose to embarrass you and clown around.

I know better.

You deserve better.

You loved hard.

My heart was barred.

Closed off.

Maybe timing could've changed this.

I wasn't ready for what you offered.

For what you give.

I need to let you go.

I have to let you go.

I need to let you be free.

Go live.

Get someone who values you.

Values your heart.

Values your mind.

Values your soul.

Someone who fits your mold.

This is what I have to say.

This is what you needed to know before I walk out of your life.

I Ain't Perfect

I ain't perfect.

A ton of flaws.

Misunderstood.

I must admit it.

I try.

I put in the time.

That alone makes me worth it.

I ain't perfect.

Mentally trapped in the midst of infidelity.

Asked, how could you?

Why would you?

What can I do?

What can I do to be the only one for you?

I ain't perfect.

All you can do is be you.

Provide a full stomach with consistent intimate sessions and hope for the best.

Pray that all you do is worth it.

I ain't perfect.

I know you deserve it.

Now our next steps through this rainfall of restoring trust is up to me.

Time Travel by Sakiya Gallon

I feel like I traveled twenty years into the past.

Where me and my family slept in the grass.

Where bloodlines cut ties and didn't last.

Where foster parents we barely knew felt like they could beat our ass.

Where I longed for nights my mom come take us back.

I used to fall asleep under stars and to the humming of cars.

We had to store our belongings in a cart, so we couldn't travel far.

I walk on the same concrete that I used to sleep.

Remembering when hunger pains made us beg for change to eat.

Separation anxiety.

The pain of missing my mother.

On cold ground we slept with the warmth of each other.

<u>Only Child, Lonely Child</u>

Have you just wanted to be understood?

Have you just been lost in yourself?

Plenty of time alone.

Momma working hard all day.

I'm home, not knowing how to handle myself while she's gone.

Attention hungry, so I might just call her phone.

Only Child, lonely child.

Mind running wild.

Imagination taking me around the globe.

Mentality molded from a young age and it set the stage.

Now lonely child is of age.

Grown up but still struggles to turn the page.

Attention daily from my homies, ladies, and family.

I still find myself closed off.

Isolated in my head, but so much love where my heart is.

Struggles of an only child.

A lonely child.

Lavish

To live lavish in any season.

Real hustler.

Living good during 2020 for no reason.

Riding around with the brand-new jeep, that's a couple months from being paid off.

Fresh off of a Mel's Exclusive carwash and detail.

$100 plus, so you can see the glare of my smile while I'm wearing the gold trimmed vintage frames.

Travel planned all through the summer through the winter.

Memphis and Chicago for September.

Phoenix for October.

Cross country to the LBC for November.

Birthday month, so I took on the expenses for my boys travel too.

A real one.

Checking out moms in the DMV for December.

I know she misses me.

All booked up.

Tithes for church going up.

Stocks steady rising.

I been going hard with this work.

I'm living good and haven't even seen a bonus yet.

Sometimes you must step down to come up.

Something I did and it took some time to recover back.

Just paid off a failed engagement ring and student loans on hold, so I got my credit back intact.

My family is healthy.

My mom just called to tell me she likes me again.

She's happy to have her son back.

How deep is that?

I've been through the hard times.

The ups and downs.

Lost it and got it back.

So, excuse me for flexing my happiness about being back on track.

It's hard to hit a moving target.

Confident brotha.

If I lose it or spend it, I know it's only a matter of time before I get it right back.

Lavish.

My lady friend is so beautiful that it's almost tragic.

When it came to her at first sight, I knew I had to have it.

Live lavish.

Love long.

Hustle hard.

Don't doubt.

What you want, God given, you can have it.

It's all a process towards living lavish.

Trust

Wishing I could give you all of me.

So scared of myself.

Scared of betraying your trust again.

The hurt in your eyes.

I can see.

Especially when it's all because of me.

Trusting you.

Letting it be what it has the potential to be.

I must make this right.

Somethings can be fixed.

Trust.

Trust can't be fixed overnight.

Life isn't right without you.

Crushed but stuck in the stubborn hold.

What can I do to prove to you?

What am I willing to do?

Trust.

Fragile.

Delicate.

But we must have it.

You've decided to let our past troubles go.

Now our next steps through the construction of restoring trust is on the clock.

Look Who It Is (Look Who I'm Fucking Again)

Look who it is.

It's been some years.

I been locked down, but I've been let free.

Brave and bold, so I hit your line just to tap in.

Shocked by the quickness on your reply time.

It hit me, that you… I never lost.

You are still mine.

I'm here in town and I'm trying to see if you're down to link up with a dude like me?

Say it ain't so.

The answer was undoubtedly yes.

The years passed by but me, she was always missing me.

For one more chance with me she was wishing.

Quietly and silently she admitted.

She made it her mission…for us to start fucking again.

Sexually our chemistry was great.

Always has been.

I ain't going to lie, for her body and intimacy I couldn't wait.

It hadn't even been a day, but she called in the AM.

5:30 to be exact and said she on her way.

Two hours later she arrived.

From the time she to touched down it was live.

For what she bestowed upon my body, I knew I had been deprived.

Her lips soft like I remember.

Her body warm, supple, and matured with time.

Down time.

She still tastes the sweetest like the cheapest Moscato wine.

Lost in how she whines and has the abnormal arch in her spine.

All I could say was, "Yeah, it's still mine."

I'm killing it without trying.

She's killing it.

We're killing it without trying.

When we are through, she lays down.

Traces every single tattoo.

That's full body.

Head to toe.

I light the spliff.

Thinking about what else I want to do to you.

By the time she finished it was time for round two.

Blue lights with the candles lit.

What a site to see, while listening to Kaash Paige playing in the background.

Listening to her word in song, I knew at least one person in this world can fully relate and feel me.

Damn...

Look who I'm fucking Again.

Brown Sugar

Back from a slight hiatus.

A mini break.

You can't block what happens to be fate.

Your brown.

Your brown skin.

Your brown skin for the win.

Your brown skin makes me want to dive in.

I took some time away, but the need of your brown skin got stronger every day.

Day by day.

With you I'll stay.

It's like being away on an adventurous vacay.

Constant reminders that home is where the heart will stay.

You say you feel less than.

Not good enough for any man.

Deep down you should know it.

You know it.

You are Queen.

You are the only one that can fully transform and understand the inner makings of me.

Your unwavering support is what I need.

You deserve the same from me.

When others put you down, like an army we should all rise and stand to our feet.

In defense of your brown sugar.

Something so pure.

Something so sweet.

Something so potent, all senses reach a peak.

Brown women.

Brown women are brown sugar.

Brown sugar isn't just to point out your delectable ray of skin, but it's something deep, rich, and undoubtedly sweet that lives within.

The Wine Down by Ambria Sylvain

Wine down my chest.

Between my breast.

Ease down my body as Marvin Gaye play while I lay.

I feel your hands.

I feel your breath from thin air.

1, 2, 3, 4....

Distant lover under my covers.

Love is blind but you are all I see.

Distant lover.

Pardon me.

Be my odyssey.

Sail my body.

Make me believe in love again.

Then I remember where I stay.

Where you are.

What I did.

Why I lay in an empty room.

Calling your name.

The blow hits my lungs.

I take the plunge deep.

2,3,4,...

Then I remember.

Marvin Gaye.

I remember why I play.

I remember you.

I am alone in this room....

Tired by Sakiya Gallon

Uncle on the corner still selling loosies.

Bull hitting my phone praying he don't lose me.

But he this close cause he pushing me away.

Yelling out for me but the streets callin his name.

Drugs staining his brain...maybe mine too.

That green keeps me up when I'm feeling down and blue.

How do you tell what's really true?

They put sugar on B.S and sell it on the news.

But look in and then look out and you'll get a clearer view.

And then finally you'll realize the truth's inside of you.

But we believe the lies.

But veils over our eyes.

Quick to make center city fly but ignore the hood and inner-city cries

But why?

Do y'all wanna see our demise?

Bullets in our backs "he had a gun" another lie?

Bull bye!

I'm tired of watching y'all whip these foreign rides.

While our blood stains our streets washed away from hard tears cried!

I'm tired!

The Playa P

Juvie at the waffle house.

She just turned eighteen.

Before I leave, she always makes sure I leave with a golden smile.

"Allstar breakfast, double waffle. I know your style."

She said, "What made you come through today? Maybe when I get off, I can come and play. Only thing is I'm working all night. Can you stay up late?"

Moving on up.

This creole blazing.

Lake Charles creole.

She's still trying to teach in her mid-thirties, but when it comes to her teacher certification, she just can't get right.

If she could get it together, we just might.

My head baby, she just like me.

She gets on her knees every night, just to pray that I remain safe and eventually become the one.

The one for her.

The attention she receives from me tends to be very slight.

A lot of ladies.

It's really to many.

When it comes to me and I have time to think about it, it's really filthy.

It becomes work, but I learn to manage.

Facetime dates scheduled, so they don't feel disconnected or like I vanished.

Lord knows, this isn't what he expected when he planned it.

The art of relationships between man and woman.

The art of finding a companion.

The Playa P who tarnished your mind and heart.

Put it in a harness.

A smooth dog, with an aggressive bite.

Never seen a muzzle he couldn't rip off when he's in a fight.

Searching for Mrs. Right or just someone to fulfill the needs of another late night.

This Ink of Mine

This ink of mine tells a story of where I was in time.

It started off as a kid with the stick of a sticker to me.

Now I rip off my shirt and ink is all you see.

My ink is me.

Uncle Kev showed me his ink and said nephew be free.

So, in my ink you see a release in me.

Me screaming, "I'm free, I'm free."

This is me.

Some appreciate the art.

Some appreciate the dedication through pain.

Some appreciate the commitment to losing your purity and never being clear again.

My ink is of course all of that.

More than anything, it is a story of my life.

My emotions.

My happiness.

My pain that will always be seen, but often never told or heard.

Never heard again by you.

Every day I hear my ink speak to me.

A constant reflection of where I used to be.

A constant reminder to keep going; you're not where you need to be yet.

Dedication.

Rise above.

Prolific.

Family first.

Live your dreams.

Loyalty.

No struggle, no pain.

Star life.

Live, hard, die young.

Memphis.

Truly missed.

Hustle.

Never back down.

These are all me.

These are all ink of mine.

Angel in The Sky

All the beautiful people that were here and have gone away.

It's crazy how when they die, you're overcome with emotion and don't know what to say.

Crying hard tears of joy on Erin's birthday.

Looking up smiling; taking in the sun's rays.

Feeling untouchable, like my dog E-way.

Hustlin' hard.

You know?

The Dump way.

Their souls leave their bodies, becoming intertwined with mine.

Forever indebted to them.

The blessings of their powers have become mine.

So much positive energy they left behind.

Granddaddy, Aunt Ellen, Uncle June, Uncle Jerry.

For them I'll forever shine.

Strength, courage, belief.

The thought that you can be whatever you want to be.

I thank Uncle Kevin for entrenching the rebel in me.

I was young but I remember him telling me, "The one thing you strive in life to be is free."

Twenty-eight was the age God took him from me.

Now I'm twenty-eight and I see how hard life can be.

So many nights I turn to these angels in the sky.

I ask them why?

Questioning and blaming God when I run astray.

Such a heathen I am, because I barely pray.

Is it wrong to think he covers me anyway?

I know I am wrong.

All the pointless shit I have going on.

It's time to change my life around.

The urge just came over me to say what I have to say.

Only one person truly knows how we feel.

So now I pray.

Bow your head.

Connect with the homage I'm about to pay.

Lord, Lord, Lord.

Thank you for covering me each day.

I know you deserve more, that's why I go to church, but from you, I feel like I run away.

Heart getting tugged, because like a stray dog, I want to play.

My sins have become overwhelming and are weighing on me.

I'm going crazy.

I know you'll save me.

I pray that you save me.

Know time for my mind to be hazy about all you've gave me.

Pride, lust, anger, frustration.

All the baggage I tend to carry.

It's only right that I let go and let God salvage me.

Lord knows, Lord knows my woes.

Angels in the sky continue to give the courage and strength to continue to try.

Lord, Lord, Lord, I apologize.

Never again will I question you or ask why.

Sight by Ambria Sylvain

Trust is actions stretched over time.

And I need more time.

To see who you move like.

What you do like?

What do you like?

How do you fight?

If you do right and I move right,

then I just might,

make that grip tight

in the midnight,

when we playfight.

Make my pen write.

Projections are for the young at heart and I fancy myself a woman.

Been chasing beats for a long time.

Switched up.

My good times, a long time coming.

So, what you feel like?

What's the deal like?

You for real-like?

Give your mind flight.

Do I make your pen write?

Just take it slow-like.

I'll let you know like.

I'll make it show…. Sight.

Black Death by Sakiya Gallon

Black man dies.

Black woman weeps.

Black people cry.

Black death creeps.

White cops shoot.

White boss meek.

Black man shot.

Blood on streets.

Black woman dies.

Black man sleeps.

Black child cries.

Black death creeps.

Blacks shoot back.

"Riots" on streets.

Black People rise.

Liberate and be free.

Damn, I Feel Good Today

Damn.

Woke up this morning feeling lite.

Weight lifted off my shoulders.

Sun shining bright.

Yesterday I questioned what I was doing.

Today I know that decision was right.

No drama.

No stress.

California beats with a row of palm trees in sight.

Today's going to be alright.

Fresh breath.

Clothes pressed.

Nails manicure, pedicured, ready to impress.

Fade tight, line straight, expect nothing less when you deal with the best.

This is what I see in the mirror.

Usually it just feels like another day.

Today it's all so much clearer.

Walking out the door ready to attack.

No fear.

Sun beaming down.

I remain cool.

Can't help but think about all the times I played the fool.

All the negative energy I was bringing behind me.

No wonder life was so cruel.

I'm no longer that way.

What can I say?

Damn, I feel good today.

Kiss My Titties by Ambria Sylvain

What about my titties nigga?

You mad?

Cause I'll still flaunt this five-star figure?

A pinch of ta-ta.

Two gallons of booty.

An ounce of clenched assed waist.

Plus this face?

A real cutie.

See, I know it.

So, what about my itsy, bitsy, little, twittle, titties?

Wittle gum drops?

Twittle spinny tops?

Dittle ding dots?

My bittle blittle blow pops?

Shut the fuck up, my nigga.

Put my shit in your mouth, my nigga.

It ain't the size of the chest that makes the woman.

With the size of my breast, I'm still more than a woman.

Still more than a woman.

I bet if I sat on your dick today, you gone keep cummin'.

I'll put these bitches in your face.

And you gone keep on suckin'.

Glowed up and showed up.

For my body type, cause it's right-like.

Respect the sensitivities of that peak time spike.

Let go and get me together.

Real quick.

Ahhhh…

Source of my afterglow.

Love of my life force.

The physical manifestation of my crowning glory.

Implore me.

To demand that….

You put some respect on my titties.

Negotiating You & Me

We started off free minded and spirited.

Open to our differences and creating a whole new experience.

We wanted to test the boundaries of love.

Love is easy.

We can make it that.

You can just be you.

Do your own thing.

Be free.
I know you love me.

It all started with communication.

Most important.

No, we don't have to talk every day for the bond to remain.

You can have all the fun with your friend.

The sex doesn't matter.

Male or female.

I get it.

We get it.

I'm not the jealous type.

I know I'm the best.

More than better than the rest.

Can you attest?

At first it was cool.

Everything was scheduled to a T.

We laid it all out.

Only at a specific time would we talk.

No random call or text from you.

Or me.

I'd come to your city, but guess what?

Your beautiful face I would not see.

If your peace and connection was off, you felt in danger with me.

Good reasoning.

The magic number was ninety days.

That's how long it would be until we could play.

Sex was on delay.

Slowly killing me.

The boundaries started off as the golden way.

Now they are breaking me down each day.

For the more we tried to stay away our yearning desire for each other got stronger.

So much stronger, I'd ponder and wonder if this could last this way any longer.

My thoughts were right.

Our bond was just too tight.

One random day we discussed how the boundaries we set were alright, but that shit had to end tonight.

I wanted you.

You wanted me.

I called you.

You called me.

I texted you.

You texted me.

Anytime it was me you wanted to see, I just caved in and let it be.

It's about time.

The sexual frustration?

We just let free.

For what is love if you can't let it grow like the oldest tree.

Caged in the confines of these boundaries of you and me.

Ball Drop

The ball drops.

You realize the moment in time stops.

Another new year.

Only difference is you're here.

New year started with a new adventure.

A southern bell getting a taste of the big apple.

Who would've thought it would be our last one?

Who could've predicted such a change in this stories plot?

Our plot.

Even when you tried to make it work, I said no.

When all our destruction was my fault.

All you could say was, why not?

Inconsiderate me.

Foolish me.

Silly me.

Thinking it was better to let you be free.

Reminiscing.

To think, this isn't the first time I let the ball drop.

1 Up Top

Thoughts of where I could've been.

Thankful that I'm not.

Thankful for everyone who've pushed me to always strive for the top.

Trials and tribulations.

Full of temptation.

Mental clouded in the things I don't got.

Can't let these times break me.

So, I wake up and continue to grind hard on the daily.

These are the times that made me.

Everything is golden.

I tend to get on my high horse.

Ferro always told me to humble myself.

The Lord will bring you back down.

Wise words.

Real love.

My brother.

Always in my corner.

For that alone,

You'll forever be in my favor.

Whatever you need.

On me.

I'm there by your side, even when you feel like I'm not.

Something special when the people you least expect are the ones pushing you.

Carrying you on their back.

A lot on my mind.

I remain at peace.

Used to want to ball and be what I thought my mom wanted me to be.

Remembering when I first tore my knee.

Sunken in defeat, because I knew she would be disappointed in me.

I was wrong.

She showed me a mother's love is too deep.

There's calmness in every storm.

Sit back.

Relax.

If this is it, it's time to really find me.

Reflection on expectations.

Expectations I thought were there and put on me, were nonexistent.

Expectations I harbored.

I put on me.

A harsh reality.

Things changed when I let them go.

Now look at me.

Free Verse From a Trapped Soul by Sakiya Gallon

Copper toned girl in a white and black world.

People question my roots because the texture of my curl.

Too focused on the branches and not enough on the root.

Get to the bottom of it and find out the truth.

The system refuses to take care of the innocent.

So, people lie on SSI just to get the benefits.

Who gone write for the niggas that are still in the field?

I'm surrounded by fakeness and still trying keep it real.

Felons got intellect.

Scholars pop shit too.

So, tell me what is a degree and some "class" going to prove?

Had knowledge before school.

My teachers made me bring it out.

In class surrounded by fools who ain't know what to say out they mouths.

Saying big words just to be heard.

I just speak from the heart and reflect on all I learn.

They get mad and conspire cause I'm speaking my mind.

Got more in common with my teachers cause their minds are just like mine.

Analyzing.

Synthesizing.

Asking questions.

Seeking answers.

Sometimes I get outta breath chasing the truth I'm after.

Is there any place in this world for a Broken Black girl?

I need to go far away for a little while so my soul can heal.

Garcia Vega

At ease.

As I break down my cannabis trees.

Bust down the green leaves.

Green leaves of the Garcia Vega.

My brain going a million miles an hour.

Thinking about if I've made my best moves yet.

Money constantly coming, but not where I want it to be.

Impatient by nature.

So, I'm already planning for what's next.

As I get lifted, I can't help but reminisce on the lives we live.

The thin lines between the haves and the have nots.

To come from a place where if you don't know how to get it.

Not familiar with the hustle.

Scared to tap in.

You'll rot slowly and anger will grow from within.

Filled with scary thoughts.

Willing to do whatever just to make it.

No thoughts of the laws.

Who cares if you get caught?

Granny said it best.

"This town is murder, murder, murder."

Murder, thieving, and violence is only natural when you're born into the life
of the have nots.

Low social economic backgrounds are the norm.

A land that refuses to have police reform.

Fathers often taken away or just decide to leave.

The village of the broken home.

We all see it.

We all know the problem.

We all have the answers.

We all think we are taking action.

When in all honestly, it's only a small fraction.

Taking another hit as I wrestle with the demons in my head.

How easily I can be the next one dead.

Innocent or guilty.

No telling how they'll get me.

I just pray that the Lord is with me.

Many put their hope in old Donald.

M.A.G.A.

All my hope is wrapped up in my thoughts.

My prayers.

In the green leaves of my last Garcia Vega.

Sliding Through This Mind of Mine

Leaving New Orleans.

Needed some time alone.

A lot going on.

Keep finding my mind is off tilt.

Stepped away.

Left my phone.

The need to be one on one with myself.

Working on my own mental health.

It's hard to do when life is always changing.

Changing faster than the seasons.

Heart broken when my auntie died.

Cancer took her body.

Corona season, so that makes everything worse.

Couldn't take seeing her in that casket like that.

Social distance was in order.

No family closeness or reassurance.

Let me know if y'all can understand my pain.

I've been dealing with a lot of petty life shit.

It would take so long to explain.

I've been ducked off for a minute.

No social media.

Phone might ring, but I pretend it's not seen.

But I'm back.

I'm out and the vibe is different.

Spirits up.

Ready to maintain.

Build Me Up: Positivity and Affection for My Crying by Ambria Sylvain

I am loving passionate and sincere.

I am honest, sometimes modest, many times unclear.

I am the treasure of all treasures they search for unawares.

I am the crim de la crop of all at the top because they need me, like they need air.

I'm fresh, honey.

Some told me, I shine so bright they couldn't understand it.

I only pray that you have the power to withstand it.

Because I wear silver lining like the finest jewelry.

Speak calamity on to chaos because peace is my second language.

I am the love of all loves because my hearts capacity is infinity.

Love coats you like Mt. Vesuvius and burns with a million suns intensity.

I am.

Beauty adorned in the deepest sense.

My mind is like oceans.

Undiscovered.

It holds no expense.

Living, giving, and fulfilling.

I am.

Thriving, rising, forever arriving.

The stars acknowledge me.

They call me "sister".

Those who don't see whisper.

"Even a blind man couldn't miss her!"

I sit amongst the highest.

Because the most-high lives in me.

Even enemies would agree.

I am the ever-essence of victory.

Flowers bloom at the presence of my energy.

And many swoon as I'm a positive entity.

All attention under my captivity.

I am.

Blazing.

Unfazed.

Eminent infinitely.

Call Me Daddy

She asked the question.

What do you want me to call you?

You know what to call me.

Do you like being called daddy?

Can I call you daddy?

Baby don't ask questions you know the answer too.

Let me tell you a secret.

I am daddy.

Don't call me anything else if you want to have me.

The look of seduction.

Biting on her lip.

I said it.

I said what I said.

She didn't trip.

She had to be mine.

She was with the shit.

The smooth grace of her voice speaking out.

"Daddy, I'm yours. Daddy, I'm yours."

She's calling me daddy.

At this point, she had me.

Enthused by her spark and confidence in her sexuality.

Handing me the dominance to see how I handled the lead.

She was strong, independent, and forthcoming in her thoughts on gender
roles and women's rights.

So, calling me daddy I thought would ignite a fight.

No matter the lady, I had to get her right.

She looked me deep into my eyes and said the words of a lifetime.

"Daddy it's alright."

Chills came through my body like a winter night.

Every time she said it, I felt myself getting stronger.

Like the most elite superhero.

I felt the power from deep within.

She's smart.

She knew the confidence it would build.

The concept of being daddy with her had me all in.

Call me daddy when we get it in.

Call me daddy to get what you want in times I refuse to bend.

Call me daddy again and again.

Call me daddy like Ice Berg Slim and Pimpin' Ken.

Call me daddy because I am him.

Cross Country Boundaries

The time has come.

I have been asked to set the record straight.

No, we aren't together.

No, we aren't in the whirlpool of monogamy.

Depending on who you ask, I guess you can say we date.

Date our way.

Nevertheless, we've decided it was time to at least start prepping for the inevitable.

We both know that we want to take our time.

That's perfectly fine.

She pushed me in the direction that these boundaries we must define.

No time for the unknown.

No time for the confusion and illusions that often show when to souls try to build a bond and become intertwined.

What should we understand about each other?

What are we not willing to give up?

At least as it pertains to this process.

First thing that comes to mind are the obvious.

See, I'm here.

She's there.

Cross country loving.

Long distance conversations will consistently have your heart tugging.

Back and forth.

How do you make this fair?

It's obvious we both care.

My mind racing with how to get my needs and wants out but keep our
courtship tight.

Topics of concern are easy but can always take a turn.

You know?

The usual.

Communication.

Sex and physical relations.

Are we free to explore and see who else is worth dating?

To make matters more complicated, we dated in the past.

I was her first and it obviously ended with major hurt and didn't last.

So, lets start this off right.

Pen to pad

Pencil to paper.

These boundaries we must have.

We made it simple, knowing eventually we will grow closer.

Changes we will have.

In bold font the paper read, BOUNDARIES.

Followed by a negotiated list.

Minimum of two Facetime dates per week.

Three at the most.

These dates will be scheduled on Sunday nights.

So, the week would be a coast.

Texting through the day is ok.

Open and transparent communication if we're feeling some type of way.

These are labeled as emergency calls.

Posting on social media isn't necessary.

Shouldn't even be a thing.

We are at peace with each other.

No sex during the first visit but after that, it's on and poppin'.

A wink and a beautiful smile from her followed.

Other sexual partners are OK, at this time.

This made sense for us at the time.

Excitement in our eyes because we knew we would be just fine.

We planned to revisit these boundaries every six week to revise.

See if we're moving closer together or wasting time.

The start of cross-country boundaries for me and mine.

Children of The System

It ain't our fault we got caught in the system.

Somebody called the people and the children fell victim.

We sulk and we suffer as we wait for fathers and mothers.

To come reclaim us from strangers who probably don't really love us.

House to house, packing up on a ninety-day notice.

Tears stain our cheeks.

No one seems to notice.

Snatch our foundation from under us, so we build up walls.

Don't want to lean on nobody.

To afraid we might fall.

I feel asleep under stars and to the humming of cards.

My mother raised her siblings because her mother stayed at bars.

Untited by Ambria Sylvain

I was bred for this.

Brought up to know your struggles.

Take on the subtitles of racism as it pertains to your gender.

To study blackness is to learn all about you.

I read you.

I breed you.

I sleep with you.

I need you.

I love you.

To be black and women means to covertly hate you.

Buried at the bottom of oppression is this simple expression.

To be black and woman is understanding that one can't step into their own power and be unconditionally loved.

My vocal outcry is your poison.

How could this be?

Talk to me.

Listen.

Please!

See, I've been in love with you all my life.

Raised to aspire someday being your wife but the older I get the harder it is for me to not see that this is the kind of life we have cut out for me.

See me.

Believe me.

Breathe the full extent if my existence.

Love me.

74

Need me.

Please kiss life into this weary spirit.

Another Day in Baton Rouge

Riding down Florida when I got the urge.

Overcome with emotion.

On the street I thought I'd never see again.

Such a beautiful city with so much pain.

The only city that can be sunny while it still rains.

This city matches me.

Reasons for feeling sane.

A home that's cut in two.

LSU and SU.

White and black.

No blend between the old and new.

Overwhelmed by the memories I have here and what I've been though.

You must be my closet homies to have a clue.

Started off in 2010.

Didn't have a clue.

Year after year.

Overtime I grew.

Fast forwarded to 2020.

Now I'm all in and remain true.

Who would've known like a flower, a man, I bloomed?

Hit my homie J and Tre'.

Crawfish boil in the spring ready.

Live it up for the day.

Hot days and pool jumping.

Things from a culture that at first seemed so strange.

Now when I'm away life ain't that same.

For Baton Rouge, a love came.

Baton Rouge a home of lifelong bonds.

Creations of multiple crews.

Brothers who took me in like family.

Joe, Josh, Dex, Tre', Jarrett, Kel.

All there for me when life was closing in on me like a jail cell.

To the Nupes.

For the krimson and kreme, no telling what I would do.

BRA is my home.

All the made Baton Rouge Nupes know the song.

Home of the beauties.

College town, so we get the women from all over the boot.

Black, white, mixed, Asian descent, and can't forget the creole.

Play around if you want to; they'll take your soul.

In the liquor section.

Albertsons on College.

Fresh out the barber chair ready to get it poppin for the night.

Store full of young ladies.

Group of white chicks but I caught the eye of the baddest one.

So, you know I'm on her tip.

I'm a nigga, but my game stays tight.

Nothing wrong with a switch up.

Came easy and correct.

She lightened to a soul that didn't seem so tough.

We walked outside.

She had a jeep like mine.

Lifted up.

She said, "I'm going to LSU and just so you know my dad's the preacher of a mega church."

Her number I got.

She left me with a hug, along with a whisper in my ear.

In a low tone, she said she know what's up.

Crazy part.

I had a girl from the start.

She never found out, but I still broke her heart.

Broke both of their hearts.

Another day in the city.

Another day in Baton Rouge.

Anxiety

Anxious with no direction or understanding of why.

Nervousness running from my head to my thighs.

My fingers tremble and sometimes I randomly want to cry.

Questioning whether I'm about to die.

My chest tightening.

I hear my heart beating slow.

I feel my heart beating fast.

My body is feeling like trash or is it about to crash?

Maybe I'm just doing the most.

Maybe I'm just living to fast.

On the outside I look fine.

I look to be normal.

Inside I feel off.

Not leveled.

Unbalanced.

I often get asked what's going on?

What's on your mind?

Why do you think you feel this way all the time?

What are you anxious about?

What do you have to be nervous about?

Questions that I struggle with and have no reply.

So, these emotions I try to hide.

Hide deep inside.

Keeping my head held high.

When I often want to put my head down and I don't know why.

Day after day I continue to get by.

Ending every night with short sputtering breaths and a deep sigh.

Undivided Attention to by Ambria Sylvain

My intentions are pure for you.

I swear it.

As pure as the poetry that you write.

As pure as the virginity that you took from me so many years ago.

Since then, I am not the same woman.

You catch me in the thick of it.

Correcting my path like a crooked spine.

Refining the curves in my choices.

The cloud of self-doubt is thick.

The closer I get to you, the scarier close gets.

I am intensely anxious.

It ain't just your honestly that did it.

It wasn't the realness you provide.

Honestly, I'm not used to this.

How twisted is that?

What is emotional vulnerability outside of myself?

No one tell me how they felt.

The journeys they've been through.

What it did for them.

Except for you.

The question isn't, "Why falling in love is so painful?"

But, "Why is painful love my comfort zone."

It is emotional vulnerability.

It is emotional inconsistency.

It is, whose love I'm still earning?

Which needs am I still yearning?

I tremble at the thought of you.

Talk, black, open, honest.

Beautiful.

Through the seduction, I barely see the finish line.

Outlined in dust are your hands to meet me.

Discomfort comes before the change.

I'll be uncomfortable for you as much as me.

Rinse through the process.

Reevaluate my mind.

Give you the undivided attention you deserve.

The Vow

Just to see you smile, makes every sunrise worthwhile.

The thought of having you makes me want to do anything.

Take that golden mile.

I'm talking wedding vowels.

So, the rest of my life I won't have to worry about ever losing sight of….
You.

One plus one equals me and you.

It will never change.

It's forever.

Us two,

That's the best math I know.

Not that I'm slow, but I'm fast to the fact that I want you.

Want you to be my last.

With so much class, unlimited potential.

Having you is essential.

Essential to my future.

Blind to the other females of my past.

All I need is the feeling of you.

Something I don't need glasses to see.

All I'm waiting on is a simple yes from you.

We can do what it do.

Me and you.

For a lifetime.

Our hearts intertwined and combined.

Please allow me your blessing.

Be mine.

How I Grew Up by Sakiya Gallon

I grew up an anomaly.

An adopted child from a close-knit family.

Two mothers.

Two fathers.

Two last names.

Remembered but forgotten.

The first child.

The last child.

The middle child.

Always the only daughter.

Knowing my mother's mother but not her father.

Knowing my father's father but not his mother.

Whole pieces with holes in them.

East and west.

North and the South.

Being furthest away from the person whose name I bare.

I wasn't supposed to be born.

Birthed and rebirthed with the world on my shoulders.

Shackles on my ankles with roses placed at my feet.

Praying to God with nails in my knees.

Holding back tears as my soul bleeds.

A swimmer who is not swift enough for the tide coming.

Thought about ocean's depth draw me nearer to it.

Like an anchor.

Drowning myself to keep others from floating away.

When the rope is cut, they drift further.

I sink deeper into the depts of solitude.

I forgot how to swim.

I imagine my mother's face, but I can't see her.

A red cardinal appears and reminds me she is near.

I listen to her.

She doesn't talk back.

I hear the sweetest notes of her voice in our favorite songs.

I breath in and imagine the smell of the last meal she cooked me.

She left me there.

I miss her presence.

But I feel her still.

Pulling me up, so I don't drown.

Pushing me along, so I don't stop and sink.

Guiding me, so I don't lose my way.

Digging in my darkness to remind me of light.

Invisible (The Black Experience)

Have you ever felt unseen?

Have you ever felt invisible?

Have you ever felt see through?

Have you ever been in a room full of people and been the life of the party?

Yet, you still felt alone?

Have you ever just thought, why am I here?

Have you ever not had the answer to that?

Have you?

Have you ever asked yourself, why is there nobody here who looks like me?

Have you ever asked yourself, why am I in this safe environment and feel like I'm in danger?

When in all rationality, everyone see's me as the main threat.

Have you ever asked, why am I the threat?

Is it because of my intelligence?

Is it because of my smartness?

Is it because of my above average good looks?

Have you ever just said, maybe I should be what they assume me to be?

But no.

What do I look like lowering my standards to their level?

Sure, you have.

I know you have.

Talk about being black in America.

Where doing right and being polite can still leave you a victim of dislike.

A victim of spite.

Well, fuck that.

I'm still going to shine.

Trust me, I'm about that life and I'm not going out without a fight.

CPSIA information can be obtained
at www.ICGtesting.com
Printed in the USA
LVHW092043121220
673819LV00041B/732